one

yī

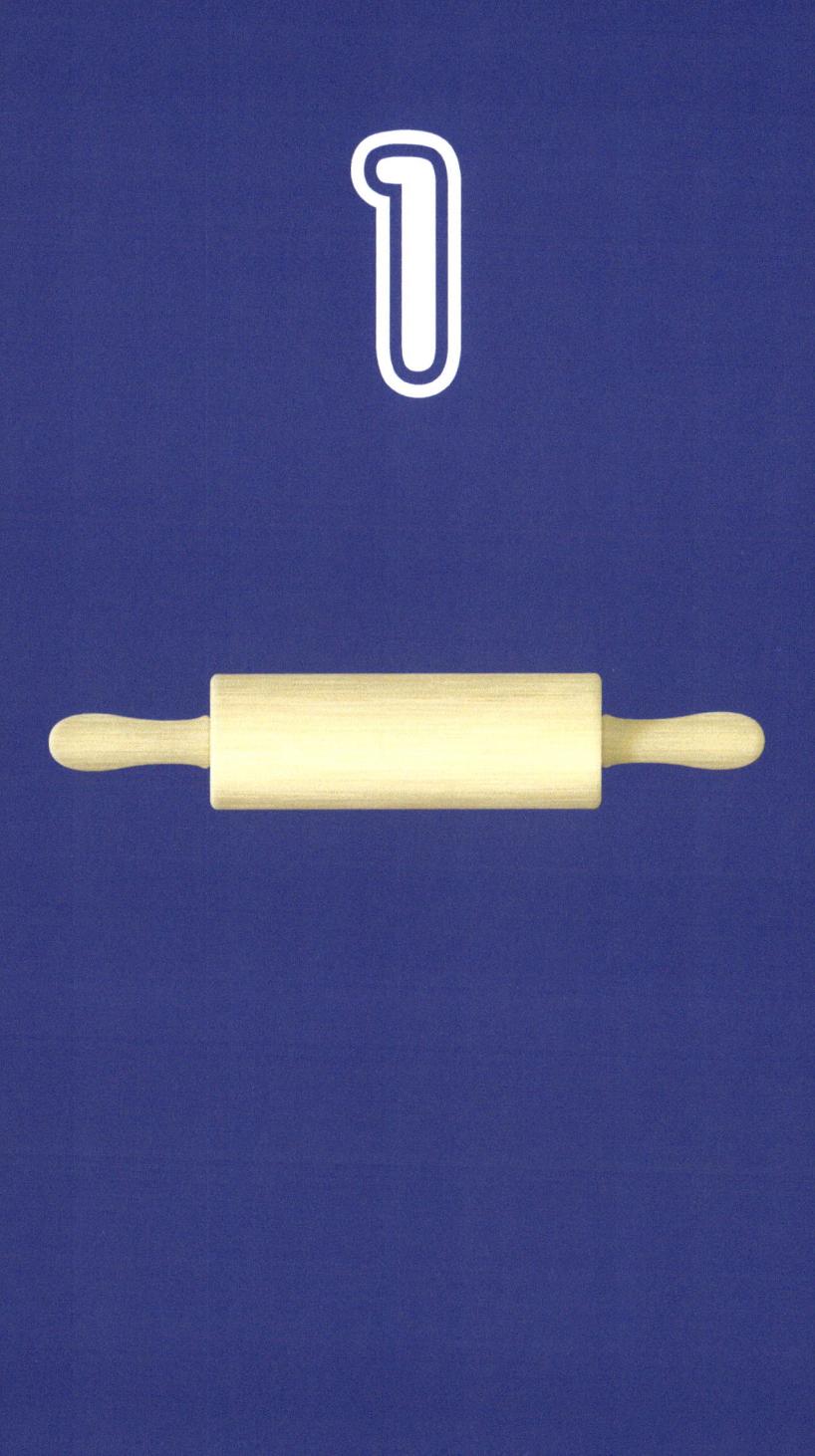

two

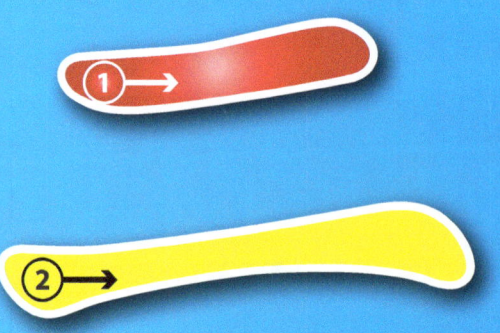

èr

2

three

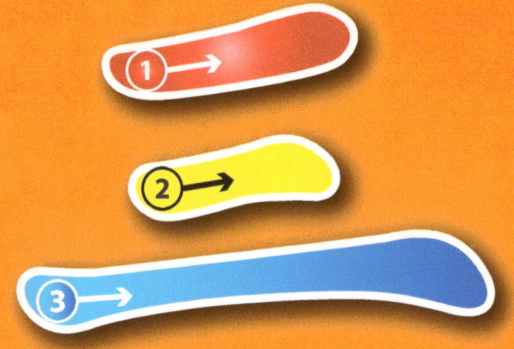

sān

four

sì

five

wǔ

six

liù

seven

qī

eight

bā

nine

jiǔ

ten

shí

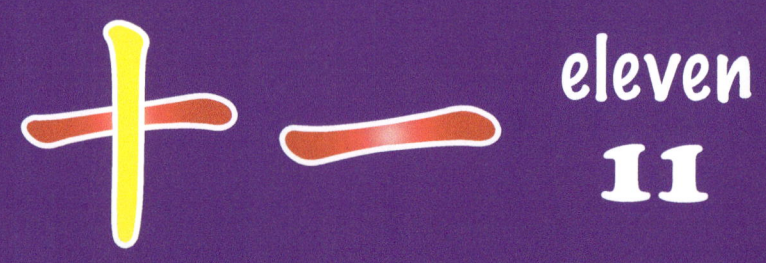

eleven
11

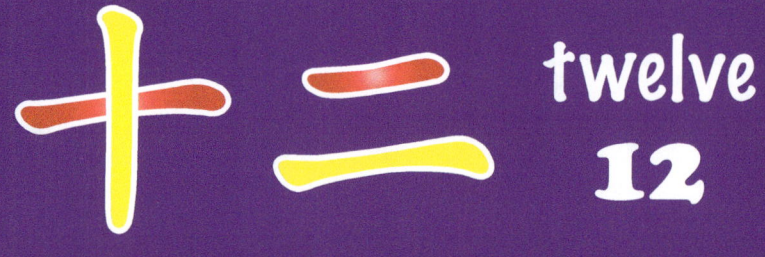

twelve
12

thirteen
13

十四 fourteen
14

十五 fifteen
15

十六 sixteen
16

www.ingramcontent.com/pod-product-compliance
Lightning Source LLC
Chambersburg PA
CBHW041452010526
44107CB00013B/1019